★ THE ★
UNITED
STATES
PRESIDENTS

HARRY S. TRUMAN

Heidi M.D. Elston

Checkerboard
Library

An Imprint of Abdo Publishing
abdobooks.com

ABDOBOOKS.COM

Published by Abdo Publishing, a division of ABDO, PO Box 398166, Minneapolis, Minnesota 55439. Copyright © 2021 by Abdo Consulting Group, Inc. International copyrights reserved in all countries. No part of this book may be reproduced in any form without written permission from the publisher. Checkerboard Library™ is a trademark and logo of Abdo Publishing.

Printed in the United States of America, North Mankato, Minnesota
052020
092020

THIS BOOK CONTAINS RECYCLED MATERIALS

Design: Emily O'Malley, Kelly Doudna, Mighty Media, Inc.
Production: Mighty Media, Inc.
Editor: Jessica Rusick

Cover Photograph: Stock Montage/Getty Images
Interior Photographs: Albert de Bruijn/iStockphoto, p. 37; AP Images, pp. 16, 29, 36; Courtesy of Harry S. Truman Library, pp. 6 (Senator Truman), 7, 11, 13, 17, 19, 27; The Crowley Company/Library of Congress, p. 25; Danita Delimont/Alamy, p. 33; Getty Images, pp. 5, 15; Hulton Archive/Getty Images, p. 31; Jim Holland/Getty Images, p. 32; Library of Congress, pp. 6 (Bess Truman), 21, 40; National Archives and Records Administration, p. 23; National Park Service, p. 12; Oscar White/Getty Images, p. 18; Pete Souza/Flickr, p. 44; Popperfoto/Getty Images, p. 20; Shutterstock Images, pp. 7 (library), 38, 39; US Air Force, pp. 7 (bombing), 22; Wikimedia Commons, pp. 6 (Truman birthplace), 10, 40 (Washington), 42

Library of Congress Control Number: 2019956561

Publisher's Cataloging-in-Publication Data

Names: Elston, Heidi M.D., author.
Title: Harry S. Truman / by Heidi M.D. Elston
Description: Minneapolis, Minnesota : Abdo Publishing, 2021 | Series: The United States presidents | Includes online resources and index.
Identifiers: ISBN 9781532193750 (lib. bdg.) | ISBN 9781098212391 (ebook)
Subjects: LCSH: Truman, Harry S., 1884-1972--Juvenile literature. | Presidents--Biography--Juvenile literature. | Presidents--United States--History--Juvenile literature. | Legislators--United States—Biography--Juvenile literature. | Politics and government--Biography--Juvenile literature.
Classification: DDC 973.918092--dc23

★ CONTENTS ★

Harry S. Truman

Harry S. Truman was the thirty-third president of the United States. He rose to this position after President Franklin D. Roosevelt died. Truman had served as Roosevelt's vice president for just 83 days.

As a young man, Truman was a farmer. He then served in the Missouri **National Guard** during **World War I**. After failing in business ventures, he turned to politics. Truman was an honest politician. He soon gained a national reputation.

In 1944, President Roosevelt decided to run for a fourth term. Truman campaigned as his **running mate**. He and Roosevelt won the election. The next year, Roosevelt died suddenly. Vice President Truman then became president.

As president, Truman made some of the hardest decisions in world history. The nation was spending billions of dollars to fight **World War II**. And, the United States had recently developed an **atomic bomb**. Truman worked hard to lead his country through this critical time.

★ TIMELINE ★

1934

Truman won election to the US Senate.

1884

On May 8, Harry S. Truman was born in Lamar, Missouri.

1922

Truman was elected a Jackson County judge.

1919

Truman married Elizabeth "Bess" Wallace on June 28.

1926

Truman was elected presiding judge of the Jackson County Court.

1941

The United States entered World War II. The US Senate established the Truman Committee to investigate defense spending.

1945

On January 20, Truman became vice president. President Roosevelt died on April 12, and Truman became president. In August, the United States dropped atomic bombs on Hiroshima and Nagasaki, Japan. World War II ended on September 2.

1949

Truman was inaugurated for his second term on January 20. The United States joined 11 countries in forming the North Atlantic Treaty Organization.

1957

The Harry S. Truman Library opened in Independence, Missouri.

★ ★   ★ ★   ★ ★

1947

Truman proposed the Truman Doctrine. Congress passed the Twenty-second Amendment. Congress also passed the Taft-Hartley Act. On July 18, Truman signed the Presidential Succession Act.

1948

On April 3, Truman signed the Marshall Plan into law. On November 2, the American people voted for Truman to continue as president.

1972

On December 26, Harry S. Truman died.

" Every segment of our population and every individual has a right to expect from our government **a fair deal.**"

HARRY S. TRUMAN

DID YOU KNOW?

★ Harry S. Truman's middle initial does not stand for anything. His parents could not decide on a middle name. It was between *Shipp*, in honor of his father's father, and *Solomon*, for his mother's father. So, Truman's parents agreed on *S* to honor both grandfathers.

★ Truman read every book in the public library in Independence, Missouri, by age 14.

★ Truman was the first president to travel underwater in a submarine.

★ Truman was the first president to give a speech on television.

★ While Truman was president, Jackie Robinson became the first African American man to play modern Major League Baseball. Robinson joined the Brooklyn Dodgers in 1947.

Missouri Beginnings

Harry's birthplace

Harry S. Truman was born on May 8, 1884, in Lamar, Missouri. He was the son of Martha Young Truman and cattle trader John Anderson Truman. Harry had a brother named John Vivian and a sister named Mary Jane.

In 1890, the Truman family moved to Independence, Missouri. There, Harry attended school. When he was about eight, Harry had to start wearing glasses. This kept him from playing sports.

At age nine, Harry caught **diphtheria**. He was sick for many weeks and had to quit school. When he got better, Harry attended summer school to catch

John and Martha Truman

up on his work. He later claimed he skipped third grade because he had studied so hard!

   Harry liked to play the piano and read. His favorite author was Mark Twain. Harry spent much of his spare time at the public library in Independence. He read many novels, history books, and encyclopedias. Harry even read the entire Bible twice before he was 12.

Harry's grandparents lived on a farm in Grandview, Missouri. During the summer, Harry and his brother and sister visited them. The children rode horses, swam, and helped with farmwork.

In high school, history was Harry's best subject. Mathilda Brown was his history teacher. She said, "I doubt if there was a student in any high school in the country who knew more of the history of the United States than Harry did."

In 1901, Harry graduated from high school. He then applied to the US Military Academy at West Point in New York. However, he was not accepted because of his poor eyesight.

The Truman family farm in Grandview

Harry then moved to Kansas City, Missouri, to look for work. There, he worked at a drugstore and the *Kansas City Star* newspaper. He was also employed by a railroad company and a bank.

After five years, Harry moved to Grandview to help run the family farm. He worked there for the next ten years. During this time, Harry tried some different business ideas. He invested in a mineral mine and an oil company. Both times, he lost his money.

In 1917, the United States entered **World War I**. At the time, Harry was still a farmer. He was also a member of the

In France, Harry and his men saw action in the Saint Mihiel and Meuse-Argonne offensives.

Missouri **National Guard**. So, in 1918, he went to France as a captain. Harry fought in several battles. He returned home in 1919.

Turning to Politics

On June 28, 1919, Truman married Elizabeth "Bess" Wallace. They had been childhood sweethearts. The Trumans had their only child on February 17, 1924. They named her Mary Margaret.

Meanwhile, Truman tried his luck at business again. In November 1919, he opened a men's clothing store in Kansas City. It made money for two years before failing in 1922.

Truman then turned to politics. A powerful politician named Tom Pendergast helped him get started. With Pendergast's support, Truman was elected a Jackson County judge in 1922. At that time, Truman entered the Kansas City Law School. For two years, he took night classes. He felt this would help his political career.

Truman ran for reelection in 1924 but lost. "I was broke and out of a job with a family to support," he later said. "But, I had a lot of friends and pulled through until 1926."

In 1926, Truman was elected **presiding judge** of the Jackson County Court. He oversaw many county expenses. Truman did his job well. He became known as an honest politician.

The Truman family

Senator Truman

In 1934, Truman decided to run for the US Senate. With Pendergast's support, Truman won the election. He took office in January 1935. Senator Truman worked hard and was honest. He soon gained people's respect. He won reelection in 1940.

Campaigning for the US Senate in 1934

The following year, the United States entered **World War II**. Truman was concerned about government money being spent on the war. He wanted to make sure this money was not wasted.

Truman asked the Senate to create the Committee Investigating the National Defense Program. This group is commonly called the Truman Committee. It was designed to stop wasteful spending.

Senator Truman

The Truman Committee helped save the US government about $15 billion. Now, Truman was one of America's best-known politicians.

The 1944 Election

In 1944, the **Democrats** chose President Franklin D. Roosevelt to run for a fourth term. But they were worried about his health. If Roosevelt died, his vice president would become president. So, he needed a strong **running mate**.

President Franklin D. Roosevelt

The Democratic Party was split. For many Democrats, current vice president Henry A. Wallace's views were too extreme. Former US **Supreme Court justice** James Byrnes was a popular choice. However, many felt he was too **conservative**. Supreme Court justice William Douglas was another favorite.

Truman was also a possible candidate. The Truman Committee investigations had earned him a national reputation. But he was happy in the Senate. President Roosevelt pressured him anyway. Finally, Truman accepted the nomination.

Roosevelt's **Republican** opponent was New York governor Thomas Dewey. Dewey's **running mate** was Ohio governor John Bricker.

Roosevelt and Truman easily won the election. Roosevelt was **inaugurated** on January 20, 1945. That day, Truman became his vice president. As vice president, Truman made no important decisions. Roosevelt rarely met with him or asked for his advice.

FROM THE DESK OF Harry S. Truman

A memo from Truman regarding the vice presidential nomination

World War II Ends

On April 12, 1945, Vice President Truman was called to the White House. There, he learned that President Roosevelt had died suddenly. By law, Truman would become the next president.

Truman took the oath of office at 7:09 p.m. Now, he faced a big challenge. Truman was not prepared to be president. But many aides helped him. Truman quickly learned how to run the nation.

Two weeks after taking office, Truman learned of a top-secret program. It was called the Manhattan Project. The US government was making an **atomic bomb**.

Meanwhile, the **Allies** were winning **World War II** in Europe. On May 7, 1945, Germany surrendered. With this, the war in Europe ended.

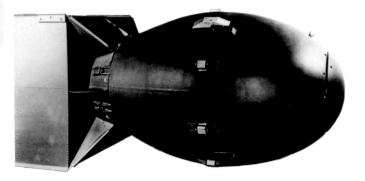

Manhattan Project members tested a plutonium bomb on July 16, 1945. It was exactly like the bomb that would later be used on Nagasaki, Japan.

US Supreme Court chief justice Harlan F. Stone
administered Truman's 1945 oath of office.

But in Asia, America was still at war with Japan. Many
people were dying every day.

Truman now faced one of the hardest decisions in world
history. He had to decide whether to use the **atomic bomb**
against Japan. Just one bomb could destroy a city.

Truman warned Japan about the bomb. He said America would use it if Japan did not stop fighting. Truman hoped this threat would force Japan to surrender. But Japan refused.

On August 6, 1945, the United States dropped an **atomic bomb** over Hiroshima, Japan. Two-thirds of the city was destroyed. Three days later, another bomb destroyed the city of Nagasaki. On September 2, Japan surrendered. Truman's tough decision took thousands of Japanese lives. Yet **World War II** was finally over.

A mushroom cloud rose above Nagasaki following the drop of an atomic bomb.

After the war, world leaders helped form the **United Nations (UN)**. Member countries agreed to work for world peace. Truman approved of the UN. So in August 1945, the US officially joined the organization.

Truman's problems in Europe were not over. Shortly after World War II ended, the **Cold War** began. **World War II** had left many countries ruined. Those countries had no money to rebuild. Now, the Soviet Union was steadily gaining control of nations in Eastern Europe.

Truman feared the Soviet Union would also take control of Greece and Turkey. He knew America needed to provide aid. So, in March 1947, he proposed the Truman Doctrine. This plan gave Greece and Turkey money to rebuild.

In June, US **secretary of state** George Marshall proposed providing money to rebuild all of Europe. This action is called the Marshall

80TH CONGRESS } HOUSE OF REPRESENTATIVES { DOCUMENT
1st Session }   { No. 171

RECOMMENDATION FOR ASSISTANCE TO GREECE AND TURKEY

ADDRESS
OF
THE PRESIDENT OF THE UNITED STATES
DELIVERED
BEFORE A JOINT SESSION OF THE SENATE AND THE HOUSE OF REPRESENTATIVES, RECOMMENDING ASSISTANCE TO GREECE AND TURKEY

MARCH 12, 1947.—Referred to the Committee on Foreign Affairs, and ordered to be printed

MR. PRESIDENT, MR. SPEAKER, MEMBERS OF THE CONGRESS OF THE UNITED STATES:
The gravity of the situation which confronts the world today necessitates my appearance before a joint session of the Congress. The foreign policy and the national security of this country are involved.
One aspect of the present situation, which I wish to present to you at this time for your consideration and decision, concerns Greece and Turkey.
The United States has received from the Greek Government an urgent appeal for financial and economic assistance. Preliminary reports from the American Economic Mission now in Greece and reports from the American Ambassador in Greece corroborate the statement of the Greek Government that assistance is imperative if Greece is to survive as a free nation.
I do not believe that the American people and the Congress wish to turn a deaf ear to the appeal of the Greek Government.
Greece is not a rich country. Lack of sufficient natural resources has always forced the Greek people to work hard to make both ends meet. Since 1940, this industrious and peace-loving country has suffered invasion, 4 years of cruel enemy occupation, and bitter internal strife.
When forces of liberation entered Greece they found that the retreating Germans had destroyed virtually all the railways, roads,

The first page of the Truman Doctrine

Plan. However, the Soviet Union would not allow Eastern European nations to receive aid. So, the plan covered only Western European nations. President Truman signed the plan into law April 3, 1948.

PRESIDENT TRUMAN'S CABINET

FIRST TERM

April 12, 1945–January 20, 1949

★ **STATE:** Edward R. Stettinius
James F. Byrnes (from July 3, 1945)
George C. Marshall (from January 21, 1947)

★ **TREASURY:** Henry Morgenthau Jr.
Frederick Moore (from July 23, 1945)
John W. Snyder (from June 25, 1946)

★ **WAR:** Henry Lewis Stimson
Robert P. Patterson (from September 27, 1945)
Kenneth C. Royall (from July 25, 1947)

★ **DEFENSE:** James V. Forrestal
(from September 17, 1947)

★ **NAVY:** James V. Forrestal

★ **ATTORNEY GENERAL:** Francis Biddle
Tom C. Clark (from July 1, 1945)

★ **INTERIOR:** Harold L. Ickes
Julius A. Krug (from March 18, 1946)

★ **AGRICULTURE:** Claude R. Wickard
Clinton P. Anderson (from June 30, 1945)
Charles F. Brannan (from June 2, 1948)

★ **COMMERCE:** Henry A. Wallace
W. Averell Harriman (from January 28, 1947)
Charles Sawyer (from May 6, 1948)

★ **LABOR:** Frances Perkins
Lewis B. Schwellenbach (from July 1, 1945)

SECOND TERM

January 20, 1949–January 20, 1953

★ **STATE:** Dean Acheson

★ **TREASURY:** John W. Snyder

★ **DEFENSE:** James V. Forrestal
Louis A. Johnson (from March 28, 1949)
George C. Marshall (from September 21, 1950)
Robert A. Lovett (from September 17, 1951)

★ **ATTORNEY GENERAL:** Tom C. Clark
J. Howard McGrath (from August 24, 1949)

★ **INTERIOR:** Julius A. Krug
Oscar L. Chapman (from January 19, 1950)

★ **AGRICULTURE:** Charles F. Brannan

★ **COMMERCE:** Charles Sawyer

★ **LABOR:** Maurice J. Tobin

President Harry S. Truman

Domestic Affairs

President Truman also faced problems in America. In 1945 and 1946, more than 1 million US workers were on strike. The workers refused to work until they were paid more money.

By June, home prices were rising. And the cost of goods such as food, clothing, and automobiles was greatly increasing. Voters blamed Truman and his fellow **Democrats**. As a result, the **Republicans** won a majority in Congress in the November elections.

In 1947, Congress passed the Twenty-second **Amendment** to the US **Constitution**. Any future president could serve only two terms or a total of ten years. The amendment did not go into effect until 1951.

Also in 1947, Congress passed the Taft-Hartley Act over Truman's **veto**. This placed limitations on labor unions. On July 18, President Truman signed the Presidential Succession Act. This altered the order of succession to the office of the US president.

President Truman kept a sign on his desk that read, "The Buck Stops Here!" This common phrase means responsibility is not passed beyond this point.

Political Upset

The year 1948 brought another election. The **Democrats** wanted to nominate General Dwight D. Eisenhower for president. However, Eisenhower refused. So, the party chose Truman instead. Senator Alben Barkley of Kentucky was his **running mate**.

Once again, the **Republicans** nominated Thomas Dewey for president. His running mate was California governor Earl Warren.

Southern Democrats who opposed the **civil rights** program of their party formed the Dixiecrat Party. They chose South Carolina governor Strom Thurmond to run for president. Mississippi governor Fielding Wright was his running mate.

Many Americans thought Dewey would win the election. But Truman campaigned hard. He traveled across the nation and gave more than 300 speeches.

The election took place November 2. Before the final results were in, radio reports declared that Truman had lost. The front page of the *Chicago Daily Tribune* read, "Dewey Defeats Truman."

Truman holds a copy of the *Chicago Daily Tribune*, which mistakenly reported he had lost the election.

However, Truman won the election with 303 electoral votes! Dewey received 189 electoral votes, and Thurmond earned 39. It was one of the biggest political upsets in US history. The **Democrats** also won control of Congress.

Foreign Affairs

On January 20, 1949, Truman was **inaugurated** for his second term. Soon after, the United States and 11 other nations formed the North Atlantic Treaty Organization. This group works to keep peace among its members. It also protects them from common enemies. At the time, one enemy was the Communist Soviet Union.

In August 1949, the Soviet Union tested an **atomic bomb**. Truman worried the Soviet Union would become more powerful than America. So, he decided the United States should make more atomic weapons. The arms race had begun.

The **Korean War** started on June 25, 1950. North Korea was a Communist country. It wanted to take over South Korea. Truman worried about the spread of Communism. He sent US soldiers to help **UN** forces defend South Korea.

US general Douglas MacArthur commanded the UN forces in Korea. Chinese Communists had

SUPREME COURT APPOINTMENTS

HAROLD H. BURTON: 1945

FRED M. VINSON: 1946

TOM C. CLARK: 1949

SHERMAN MINTON: 1949

More than 50,000 American soldiers
died during the Korean War.

joined North Korea in the fighting. So, MacArthur wanted
to launch an attack on China. But Truman wanted to keep
the fighting in North Korea. MacArthur publicly criticized
Truman. In April 1951, Truman removed MacArthur from his
command. The war ended in 1953.

Truman Goes Home

From 1948 to 1952, the White House was under construction. So, President Truman and his family lived in Blair House. It was across the street from the White House.

In retirement, Truman remained active in politics.

On November 1, 1950, Truman survived an **assassination** attempt at Blair House. After the incident he said, "A president has to expect those things." He conducted his usual business that day.

In 1952, Truman decided not to run for reelection. He retired to his home in Independence, Missouri, the following year. There,

While in office, the president receives a salary of $400,000 each year. He or she lives in the White House and has 24-hour Secret Service protection.

The president may travel on a Boeing 747 jet called Air Force One. The airplane can accommodate 76 passengers. It has kitchens, a dining room, sleeping areas, and a conference room. It also has fully equipped offices with the latest communications systems. Air Force One can fly halfway around the world before needing to refuel. It can even refuel in flight!

Air Force One

If the president wishes to travel by car, he or she uses Cadillac One. It has been modified with heavy armor and communications systems. The president takes

Cadillac One

Cadillac One along when visiting other countries if secure transportation will be needed.

The president also travels on a helicopter called Marine One. Like the presidential car, Marine One accompanies the president when traveling abroad if necessary.

Sometimes, the president needs to get away and relax with family and friends. Camp David is the official presidential retreat. It is located in the cool, wooded mountains of Maryland. The US Navy maintains the retreat, and the US Marine Corps keeps it secure. The camp offers swimming, tennis, golf, and hiking.

When the president leaves office, he or she receives lifetime Secret Service protection. He or she also receives a yearly pension of $207,800 and funding for office space, supplies, and staff.

Marine One

	PRESIDENT	PARTY	TOOK OFFICE
1	George Washington	None	April 30, 1789
2	John Adams	Federalist	March 4, 1797
3	Thomas Jefferson	Democratic-Republican	March 4, 1801
4	James Madison	Democratic-Republican	March 4, 1809
5	James Monroe	Democratic-Republican	March 4, 1817
6	John Quincy Adams	Democratic-Republican	March 4, 1825
7	Andrew Jackson	Democrat	March 4, 1829
8	Martin Van Buren	Democrat	March 4, 1837
9	William H. Harrison	Whig	March 4, 1841
10	John Tyler	Whig	April 6, 1841
11	James K. Polk	Democrat	March 4, 1845
12	Zachary Taylor	Whig	March 5, 1849
13	Millard Fillmore	Whig	July 10, 1850
14	Franklin Pierce	Democrat	March 4, 1853
15	James Buchanan	Democrat	March 4, 1857
16	Abraham Lincoln	Republican	March 4, 1861
17	Andrew Johnson	Democrat	April 15, 1865
18	Ulysses S. Grant	Republican	March 4, 1869
19	Rutherford B. Hayes	Republican	March 3, 1877

George Washington

Abraham Lincoln

Theodore Roosevelt

LEFT OFFICE	TERMS SERVED	VICE PRESIDENT
March 4, 1797	Two	John Adams
March 4, 1801	One	Thomas Jefferson
March 4, 1809	Two	Aaron Burr, George Clinton
March 4, 1817	Two	George Clinton, Elbridge Gerry
March 4, 1825	Two	Daniel D. Tompkins
March 4, 1829	One	John C. Calhoun
March 4, 1837	Two	John C. Calhoun, Martin Van Buren
March 4, 1841	One	Richard M. Johnson
April 4, 1841	Died During First Term	John Tyler
March 4, 1845	Completed Harrison's Term	Office Vacant
March 4, 1849	One	George M. Dallas
July 9, 1850	Died During First Term	Millard Fillmore
March 4, 1853	Completed Taylor's Term	Office Vacant
March 4, 1857	One	William R.D. King
March 4, 1861	One	John C. Breckinridge
April 15, 1865	Served One Term, Died During Second Term	Hannibal Hamlin, Andrew Johnson
March 4, 1869	Completed Lincoln's Second Term	Office Vacant
March 4, 1877	Two	Schuyler Colfax, Henry Wilson
March 4, 1881	One	William A. Wheeler

Franklin D. Roosevelt

John F. Kennedy

Ronald Reagan

	PRESIDENT	PARTY	TOOK OFFICE
20	James A. Garfield	Republican	March 4, 1881
21	Chester Arthur	Republican	September 20, 1881
22	Grover Cleveland	Democrat	March 4, 1885
23	Benjamin Harrison	Republican	March 4, 1889
24	Grover Cleveland	Democrat	March 4, 1893
25	William McKinley	Republican	March 4, 1897
26	Theodore Roosevelt	Republican	September 14, 1901
27	William Taft	Republican	March 4, 1909
28	Woodrow Wilson	Democrat	March 4, 1913
29	Warren G. Harding	Republican	March 4, 1921
30	Calvin Coolidge	Republican	August 3, 1923
31	Herbert Hoover	Republican	March 4, 1929
32	Franklin D. Roosevelt	Democrat	March 4, 1933
33	Harry S. Truman	Democrat	April 12, 1945
34	Dwight D. Eisenhower	Republican	January 20, 1953
35	John F. Kennedy	Democrat	January 20, 1961

LEFT OFFICE	TERMS SERVED	VICE PRESIDENT
September 19, 1881	Died During First Term	Chester Arthur
March 4, 1885	Completed Garfield's Term	Office Vacant
March 4, 1889	One	Thomas A. Hendricks
March 4, 1893	One	Levi P. Morton
March 4, 1897	One	Adlai E. Stevenson
September 14, 1901	Served One Term, Died During Second Term	Garret A. Hobart, Theodore Roosevelt
March 4, 1909	Completed McKinley's Second Term, Served One Term	Office Vacant, Charles Fairbanks
March 4, 1913	One	James S. Sherman
March 4, 1921	Two	Thomas R. Marshall
August 2, 1923	Died During First Term	Calvin Coolidge
March 4, 1929	Completed Harding's Term, Served One Term	Office Vacant, Charles Dawes
March 4, 1933	One	Charles Curtis
April 12, 1945	Served Three Terms, Died During Fourth Term	John Nance Garner, Henry A. Wallace, Harry S. Truman
January 20, 1953	Completed Roosevelt's Fourth Term, Served One Term	Office Vacant, Alben Barkley
January 20, 1961	Two	Richard Nixon
November 22, 1963	Died During First Term	Lyndon B. Johnson

	PRESIDENT	PARTY	TOOK OFFICE
36	Lyndon B. Johnson	Democrat	November 22, 1963
37	Richard Nixon	Republican	January 20, 1969
38	Gerald Ford	Republican	August 9, 1974
39	Jimmy Carter	Democrat	January 20, 1977
40	Ronald Reagan	Republican	January 20, 1981
41	George H.W. Bush	Republican	January 20, 1989
42	Bill Clinton	Democrat	January 20, 1993
43	George W. Bush	Republican	January 20, 2001
44	Barack Obama	Democrat	January 20, 2009
45	Donald Trump	Republican	January 20, 2017

Barack Obama

★ PRESIDENTS MATH GAME ★

Have fun with this presidents math game! First, study the list above and memorize each president's name and number. Then, use math to figure out which president completes each equation below.

1. Harry S. Truman – William Taft = ?

2. John Tyler + Harry S. Truman = ?

3. Harry S. Truman – Thomas Jefferson = ?

Answers: 1. John Quincy Adams (33 – 27 = 6)
2. George W. Bush (10 + 33 = 43)
3. Calvin Coolidge (33 – 3 = 30)

LEFT OFFICE	TERMS SERVED	VICE PRESIDENT
January 20, 1969	Completed Kennedy's Term, Served One Term	Office Vacant, Hubert H. Humphrey
August 9, 1974	Completed First Term, Resigned During Second Term	Spiro T. Agnew, Gerald Ford
January 20, 1977	Completed Nixon's Second Term	Nelson A. Rockefeller
January 20, 1981	One	Walter Mondale
January 20, 1989	Two	George H.W. Bush
January 20, 1993	One	Dan Quayle
January 20, 2001	Two	Al Gore
January 20, 2009	Two	Dick Cheney
January 20, 2017	Two	Joe Biden
		Mike Pence

★ WRITE TO THE PRESIDENT ★

You may write to the president at:

**The White House
1600 Pennsylvania Avenue NW
Washington, DC 20500**

You may email the president at:

www.whitehouse.gov/contact

★ GLOSSARY ★

allies—people, groups, or nations united for some special purpose. During World War II Great Britain, France, the United States, and the Soviet Union were called the Allies.

amendment—a change to a country's constitution.

assassination—the act of murdering a very important person, usually for political reasons.

atomic bomb—a bomb that uses the energy of atoms. It is thousands of times more powerful than a regular bomb.

civil rights—rights that protect people from unequal treatment or discrimination.

Cold War—a period of tension and hostility between the United States and its allies and the Soviet Union and its allies after World War II.

conservative—of or relating to a political philosophy based on tradition and preferring gradual development to abrupt change.

Constitution—the laws that govern the United States.

Democrat—a member of the Democratic political party. Democrats believe in social change and strong government.

diphtheria (dihp-THIHR-ee-uh)—a disease that affects the throat and can cause death.

inaugurate (ih-NAW-gyuh-rayt)—to swear into a political office.

justice—a judge on the US Supreme Court.

Korean War—from 1950 to 1953. A war between North and South Korea. The US government sent troops to help South Korea.

National Guard—one of the voluntary military organizations of the US Army and Air Force. Each state, most territories, and the District of Columbia has its own National Guard. Each unit is commanded by individual state governors and the president.

presiding judge—the judge that manages the county courts and their schedules. He or she also appoints judges to specialized courts and oversees meetings of the judges.

Republican—a member of the Republican political party. Republicans are conservative and believe in small government.

running mate—a candidate running for a lower-rank position on an election ticket, especially the candidate for vice president.

secretary of state—a member of the president's cabinet who handles relations with other countries.

Supreme Court—the highest, most powerful court in the United States.

United Nations (UN)—a group of nations formed in 1945. Its goals are peace, human rights, security, and social and economic development.

veto—the right of one member of a decision-making group to stop an action by the group. In the US government, the president can veto bills passed by Congress. But Congress can override the president's veto if two-thirds of its members vote to do so.

World War I—from 1914 to 1918, fought in Europe. Great Britain, France, Russia, the United States, and their allies were on one side. Germany, Austria-Hungary, and their allies were on the other side.

World War II—from 1939 to 1945, fought in Europe, Asia, and Africa. Great Britain, France, the United States, the Soviet Union, and their allies were on one side. Germany, Italy, Japan, and their allies were on the other side.

ONLINE RESOURCES

Booklinks
NONFICTION NETWORK
FREE! ONLINE NONFICTION RESOURCES

To learn more about Harry S. Truman, please visit **abdobooklinks.com** or scan this QR code. These links are routinely monitored and updated to provide the most current information available.

★ INDEX ★